D1098087

A LITTLE BIT

OF

SYMBOLS

A LITTLE BIT

OF

SYMBOLS

AN INTRODUCTION
TO SYMBOLISM

HENRY REED

STERLING ETHOS
New York

STERLING ETHOS
New York

An Imprint of Sterling Publishing Co., Inc.
1166 Avenue of the Americas
New York, NY 10036

STERLING ETHOS and the distinctive Sterling logo are registered
trademarks of Sterling Publishing Co., Inc.

Text © 2016 by Henry Reed

All rights reserved. No part of this publication may be reproduced, stored in a retrieval system, or
transmitted in any form or by any means (including electronic, mechanical, photocopying, recording,
or otherwise) without prior written permission from the publisher.

ISBN 978-1-4549-1969-8

Distributed in Canada by Sterling Publishing Co., Inc.
℅ Canadian Manda Group, 664 Annette Street
Toronto, Ontario, Canada M6S 2C8
Distributed in the United Kingdom by GMC Distribution Services
Castle Place, 166 High Street, Lewes, East Sussex, England BN7 1XU

For information about custom editions, special sales, and premium and corporate purchases,
please contact Sterling Special Sales at 800-805-5489 or specialsales@sterlingpublishing.com.

Manufactured in the United States of America

2 4 6 8 10 9 7 5 3 1

www.sterlingpublishing.com

CONTENTS

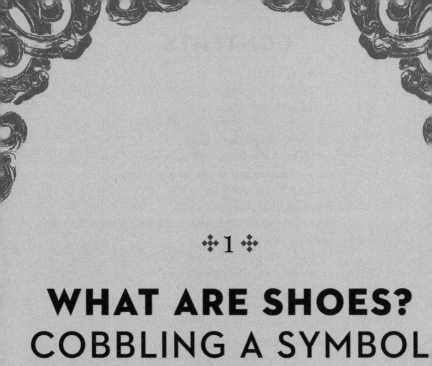

✤ 1 ✤

WHAT ARE SHOES?
COBBLING A SYMBOL
FROM EVERYDAY LIFE

I HAD A DREAM THAT SPARKED AN EXPERIMENT IN exploring symbolism.

In my dream, I opened my closet and a torrent of shoes poured out upon the floor.

At the time of this dream, I did have a lot of shoes. I have fewer shoes now, having refined my needs and preferences. I remain a shoe enthusiast, nevertheless. Just as the right tool for the right job makes all the difference, having the right pair of shoes for a given situation does provide a distinct advantage.

To have such an abundance of shoes appear in my dream made me ask, "What do shoes mean?" As we'll come to appreciate, context is everything. That context is our relationship to shoes and their characteristics—it's there that we find the meaning that shoes have for us.

Can we understand the meaning of something, I wondered,

by observing how it appears or behaves in our dreams? To test this idea, I placed an ad in a magazine likely read by dreamers, asking for dreams about shoes. It didn't take long before I had received in reply almost two hundred dreams involving shoes.

I analyzed the dreams, studying the way shoes made their cameo appearances.

The most frequent pattern was a dreamer finding shoes, or searching for shoes, with special features. Dreamers found shoes made of volcanic ash, for example; or shoes made from living, walking turtles; shoes with wings; and high-heeled tennis shoes. These dreams are reminiscent of fairy tales involving special shoes, such as Hans Christian Andersen's story "The Red Shoes," the magic shoes worn by Dorothy in *The Wizard of Oz*, or the winged sandals of the Roman god Mercury.

The second most common theme in the dreams I analyzed was a pervasive concern about the appropriateness of the shoes being worn. One dreamer tried to walk through snow in high heels. Ronald Reagan sold another dreamer a pair of shoes the dreamer wasn't sure she really wanted. One dreamer complained that the shoes didn't fit appropriately; they were too tight. Another dreamer wore tennis shoes to a fancy ball.

The third most frequent theme was that of losing one's shoes. One dreamer left a party and later discovered that she had left her shoes behind. Someone took another dreamer's shoes. One dreamer was standing in line at a complaint department to describe shoes that had been lost. Another dreamer was riding on a horse when his shoes fell off.

Many dreams involved shopping for shoes. A particular challenge is to find a pair of shoes that are both appropriate to the outer situation (including appearance and fashion) as well as comfortable and supportive of the inner situation—the emotional tenor of the person wearing them.

Discovering old shoes was another favorite, as well as losing the mate to a needed shoe.

Shoe dreams seem to mirror the shoe situations encountered in life. Shoes with special features seem to be a notable exception.

Do an Internet search for "shoes symbol," and perhaps the most common description is "understanding." Other explanations for the shoe as symbol include the terms *role*, *adaptation*, and *persona*. It's as if to say, the kind of shoes one wears expresses one's understanding of a situation, the approach taken to the situation, the way one adapts to it, or the role taken in the situation.

I might add that shoes represent understanding also in the sense of them being cognitive schemes, or mental abstractions, used as structures to contain and give shape to experience. They are tools in consciousness used as an adaptive tool to help navigate through life situations.

The general notion provided through the Internet search for shoe symbolism (i.e., that shoes represent understanding, as an attitude, strategy, or approach) is not far from the conclusions reached by this research. But perhaps there's more.

Many shoe dreams reflected a concern for individuality as well as appropriateness. In one dream, for example, the dreamer lamented that all the shoes in the store seemed mass produced and none fit her unique orientation. One dreamer offered this observation, which can be taken both literally and metaphorically: "It's hard to find a good-looking pair of shoes that fit comfortably."

"One size fits all" is definitely *not* what shoes are about. There's the outside of shoes, and how they look and how they adapt. But then there's the inside of shoes, and how they fit or feel to the person wearing them. To "walk in someone's shoes" means to empathize with that person, with the *inside feel* of that person. Here the shoe symbol brings up an important dimension of universal human experience: how we appear to others and get along versus how we feel, as individuals, on the inside. We want to find a way to be comfortable with ourselves and, at the same time, fit in comfortably with others.

Given this concern for functional and appropriate shoes that match the dreamer's individuality, it is surprising that in none of the dreams was there ever mention of making one's own shoes or having custom-made shoes. Here is an aspect of shoes from real life that is missing in dreams. What can explain this discrepancy? Is it simply because I didn't collect enough shoe dreams?

Perhaps it is because the types of understanding symbolized by shoes aren't the sort we consciously design or create but come ready-made from the unconscious mind. For example, in fairy tales, it is often the Brownies that make shoes for a person while that person sleeps. In this case, the understanding that shoes represent may come in the form of an inspiration or creative idea upon awakening. In any case, we will need to explore the mystery of where symbols come from and how they are created.

In some sense, then, shoes, as a symbol, can represent something about symbolism itself. Shoes provide for a relationship between our conscious standpoint and something "other," such as the physical environment or a social situation. That symbols exist is in itself a clue that there's more to this world than we realize consciously. There is something for us to understand. Symbols thus offer a relationship between what is known and what is generally unknown, an approach to the unconscious or greater mind. We might ask, then, "What kind of shoes might be best to wear when we go to explore symbols?"

At the end of each chapter there are a few pictures. They, and the captions accompanying them, exist not as a miniature dictionary or encyclopedia of symbolism. Instead, they present themselves to stimulate your imagination. They give you some practice exploring and discovering how symbols can lead you into interesting experiences and ideas.

The captions give you a start into the process. The captions, however, are words, not symbols. The words can't substitute for the experiences latent within the symbol. Like the finger pointing to the moon, the finger isn't the moon itself. The only connection is that the finger is pointing to the sky, where you can see the moon. Even then, the finger is pointing in the correct direction only half of the day, for during the other half day, the moon is below us. So words only approximate, and only some of the time.

Notice what thoughts and feelings come to you as you recall some of the attributes of the symbol. Looking at a shoe, for example, we think about how it fits on our foot and how it makes our foot feel. Suppose you had wings on your shoes; how would that feel? What if your shoes had wheels under them; how would that affect how you walk about? Where does that take your imagination? Go for a stroll in each pair of shoes and see where each pair takes you, and how.

Enjoy symbolism like a wonderful dessert, rather than like a crossword puzzle.

SOME SYMBOLS TO SAMPLE

If you had wings on your shoes, you'd . . .

Imagine walking on tiptoes.

Want to go bear foot?

Just rolling along . . .

THE BRAIN ON SYMBOLS:

STRATEGIES FOR EXPLORING A LITTLE SYMBOLISM

I N THIS BOOK WE WILL EXPLORE A BRIEF OVERVIEW
of what symbols can mean to us and how best to use that knowledge to our advantage. My dream of shoes arrived while I was
in psychoanalysis. That work, together with my own practice as a
psychotherapist, gave me firsthand experience with the value of
symbolism for uncovering parts of ourselves we'd never expect. As
a university professor, I researched with students how to create edu-
cational exercises for exploring these regions of the mind. Working
with the support of members of Edgar Cayce's Association for
Research and Enlightenment, I created, researched, and published
intuitive methods for expanding consciousness through symbolism.

Let's begin by looking at what we mean by symbolism. There
now exists something akin to a science of *symbolism* that recognizes
certain principles. The first principle is that a symbol points beyond
itself. It is an invitation to experience something new. To hear the

phrase "this symbol means . . . " and then hear the judge's gavel strike—that is not the experience of symbolism. Instead, symbolism is more like having an *ah-ha!* moment and marveling at the new thoughts and experiences suddenly becoming apparent.

To gain a better feeling for symbols, consider something that happens with dreams. First, imagine a child playing with a ball in the front yard while the parents watch from the porch. The ball rolls out into the street, and the child impulsively runs after it. Seeing the danger causes the parents to involuntarily emit a warning cry for the child to hear. Waking up from a dream is much like the child's hearing an unsettling, loud noise of warning from the parents, which may or may not slow or stop the child in its tracks. The purpose of a dream seems to be to create in the conscious mind some empathy—even if not consciously understood—for the greater perspective of the unconscious (or Mind-of-God).

A symbol functions to inspire in the conscious mind some degree of empathy for the perspective of the greater unconscious mind. Symbols of long standing in human history express intuitive insights about the human condition. Symbols arising from personal experience, often countered in dreams, function to stimulate new insights about our current relationship to life events.

Rather than thinking in terms of categories, such as "this is a symbol; that is not," we want to learn to think in terms of function: "Here X is functioning as a symbol; here it is not." Something is functioning as a symbol, for example, when its purpose is the expanding or evolving of consciousness. Sometimes the symbolic function shapes behavior, perhaps ominously, while the awareness aspect seems lagging.

Something is acting as a symbol if it stimulates us beyond our will and understanding. Ideally, developing a relationship to a symbol's mystery will stimulate an expansion of consciousness.

Symbols are pregnant with meaning, yet they do not "mean" specifically this or that. Symbols are certainly suggestive, if nothing else, but they do not "signify" something in particular like a sign does. Symbols are certainly used in lieu of explicit understanding, yet their use does not "equate" with something that can be specified. When something "symbolizes," it evokes thoughts and intuitions of connections between different areas of life. When something is active as a symbol, it is teasing out new realizations. A symbol shares its perspective slowly at the evolutionary rate of "when the student is ready, the teacher will appear."

That same something is not functioning as a symbol when its purpose is to serve as a substitute, or representative, for something that is already known, identified, or understood, or when it is being treated as if its meaning were so specifically anchored. There are many symbol-like tools that we use as shorthand codes; for example, the dollar sign and the symbols in math and science or in music. Sometimes in literature or the arts, we use objects to represent or suggest other ideas or concepts. We can interpret these signs. Symbols, on the other hand, tease and confound interpretation, preferring to get under our skin, on our brain, and in our heart, stimulating our imagination. Symbols weren't designed to provide closure—their purpose is to open new possibilities.

Dreaming of a flood of shoes gushing from my closet certainly stimulated my curiosity about the symbolic meaning of shoes. Here I was confronted by the essential challenge with regard to symbolism—how do I gain the expanded awareness that a symbol is stimulating in me?

Earlier I wondered, "What kind of shoes would be best for exploring the world of symbols?" Slippers are comfortable on the feet, that is, unless the terrain gets rough. The advantage of a good pair of hiking boots is that they provide a type of comfort that doesn't deteriorate in rough terrain. If our interest in the meaning of a symbol is casual, and we intend to stay in our comfort zone, we may find slippers adequate to the task of understanding the symbol. An easy, maybe lazy approach to satisfying a casual curiosity about the meaning of a symbol would be to look it up in our favorite symbol dictionary, or to google the meaning. In either case, we can thus enjoy the cozy feeling we get when we read about something interesting that expands our knowledge.

If we have a personal stake in the symbol—such as because of a recurrent dream—we may no longer be satisfied with the simple comfort of a pair of slippers but may aspire to understanding that requires sturdy hiking boots, as we will wish to maintain confidence as we explore some unfamiliar and perhaps uncomfortable ideas, feelings, or memories. As we learn various approaches and methods for exploring a symbol from within, we will require the inner stability of affirming our intention or purpose, while also having the flexibility to allow uncommon streams of thought to occur and be noticed in some detail. Such inner explorations of the meaning of a symbol, especially when it has been following us around, will take us beyond our zone of familiar knowledge. Yet, the more we travel in those domains, the more comfortable we become with "not knowing and still learning," so our understanding can continue to evolve.

I responded to the shoe symbol from my dream in two ways. I asked myself, "What do shoes mean to me?" I also began to do some research on shoes. In other words, I looked both within myself as well as outwardly. We need to be prepared to do both if we want to have a meaningful relationship to symbolism.

The "hermeneutical" tradition, named after the Greek god Hermes, concerns the philosophy and science of interpretation and wisdom. Among its principles, outlined in the often-cited, yet controversial text *The Kybalion: A Study of The Hermetic Tradition of Ancient Egypt and Greece*, is the principle of "correspondence." This idea, usually stated as "as Above, so Below," refers to how the inner world mirrors the outer, how Earth mirrors Heaven, how the human mirrors All of creation, and how each and every of the many individual things mirror the underlying, Unitary source—"the Many are One."

The purpose or function of symbolism is to grow consciousness, expanding awareness of such important truths about life. When we find something stimulating our interest, stirring our imagination, perhaps there is a symbolic dimension involved. We stand to learn something about ourselves and our relationship to life by exploring that symbol. Our goal is not to find and stop at the symbol's interpretation, but by following the path of the symbol's enchantment, we aim to become aware of relationships and connections previously ignored or unconscious. We'll find that symbols become more real and alive as we allow them to make a difference in how we perceive, understand, and respond to our world.

SOME SYMBOLS TO SAMPLE

Feel the sun on
your face . . .

What's it like to be
stared at?

How can something good come
from something that hurts?

What are we agreeing to?

✢ 3 ✢

LET THE CIRCLE
BE UNBROKEN:

EMBRACING
A UNIVERSAL
SYMBOL

T HE MIND'S SEARCH FOR MEANING IS WHERE symbolism comes into play.

Outside of ourselves exist the "facts" available to our sense perception. These "facts" are objectively observable. Most other people using the same method to observe the world will agree on these facts. It's within us, however, that we explore the intuitions of meaning concerning our experiences.

It's one thing to look around and study how the universe functions. But it's another thing to wonder about *why* the universe has come to exist or about the *purpose* or *meaning* of our *experiences*.

Let's start at the beginning. The beginning is a *big mystery*! How did it all begin? Where did we come from? How did we get here? Why are we here?

How have we explained this mystery to ourselves? What's the story?

The science of physics, with its atoms and forces, provides an explanation of the big bang! Out of apparently "nothing" there was an explosion of stars that then spread out in all directions to form a universe. But that's all about "things" moving, colliding, and changing. What about the fact of awareness itself, consciousness, that mystery that distinguishes sentient beings from inanimate things? Our knowledge of the big bang provides some answers to the question "How does the universe work?" But it doesn't answer the question "Why is it here?"

To answer the question "What's the story?" we have old myths. We understand that creation myths are full of symbolism. To gain a deeper understanding of creation myths, let's use our imagination to explore the symbolism of a symbol that is pervasive throughout these stories—the circle.

Let's imagine creating a circle by opening our arms, bending our elbows, and joining our fingertips, as if we were wrapping our arms around something big. Notice how the arms embrace all that is within that circle. Imagine the space created by our encircling arms and how that space is empty. Get a feeling for the circle we have created as suggesting two different things simultaneously—it contains everything and it is empty at the same time.

Employing physical empathy for the circle with our arms allows the circle symbolism—its emptiness but also its potential—to begin to cast its spell. The best way to think symbolically is not to think in terms of interpretation—what does it *mean*?—but to instead ask,

"Where does it take me?" In what other way might we use our body to express the idea of the circle? By going inside of ourselves, meditatively and with intent, we can reap the reward of inner knowledge that the symbol elicits.

Begin to think of yourself as a circle, empty but containing everything. When I begin to pretend that *I am* a circle, I want to look around. Then the phrase comes to me: "all around." When I think *about* a circle, phrases occur to me such as "the circle of life" or "the great round of being." I think about the circle having a center, and everywhere around it is the edge of its being. Making a complete circle, coming full circle, the cycle of the seasons, the cycle of life. The circle seems to enclose everything.

I see people standing in a large circle, holding hands. I see people dancing in a circle. The circle suggests that we are all connected as a *single being*.

There are many examples from the world's cultural heritage that express aspects of the circle's symbolism. When I begin an Internet search for "circle symbolism," there is one image result that is quite striking. It is that of the snake biting its tail to form a circle. The name given to this symbol is *ouroboros*. It expresses an intuition about what the world was like before there was any awareness of it.

The ouroboros symbol expresses a certain realization about creation as a self-contained cycle of one physical thing transforming through ingestion into something else. It is a picture of the circle of life as a giant food chain feeding on itself, yet "empty" of awareness—nobody is home but the mechanisms and instincts needed to keep the circle going. The *ouroboros* shows us that there is a difference between the operation of the physical universe and the awareness of its existence.

What is the source of such a symbol? In a book inspired by the perspective of Edgar Cayce, *Sacred Geometry and Spiritual Symbolism: The Blueprint for Creation*, Donald B. Carroll describes that source as the universal unconscious mind, deep within us all. I use Edgar Cayce's term and call this mysterious source the Mind-of-God. It's my way of noting a special correspondence between the intelligent design apparent in the physical universe and patterns in the mind. It also reflects accumulating wisdom that this source has the intent and purpose to become more conscious by reflecting on its action via symbolism.

The *ouroboros* symbol is a communication from the Mind-of-God suggesting a creation that existed before time as we know it began. If we were to continue our online research into the circle symbolism, we would encounter ideas such as the circle being *the* symbol for the divinity.

Here are some interesting aspects of the circle that are divinely suggestive. First, God has been known to be centered everywhere and extending beyond forever. In this perspective, the circle expresses aspects of God that are beyond thinking, that are irrational. Mathematicians discovered long ago that to calculate the area contained by a circle, we must resort to the "irrational" number pi, suggesting that we can only get so far with objective thinking about God, and then we must turn inward to the subjective imagination.

When symbolizing wholeness, there is also implicit in the circle the notion of the cycle, the eternal return. There is the cycle of the seasons, which makes creative growth possible. So the theme of death and rebirth is present as well. It's all there in the circle; wrap our arms around it all, and we get the feeling for the circle's symbolic pull.

What makes a symbol universal is that it has many diverse examples. The circle "archetype" expresses itself in many diverse ways across time and cultures. The archetype is the underlying, unifying source of the symbol's many expressions. As the mythologist Joseph Campbell noted, the "hero" (that's the archetype) has a "thousand faces" (those are the various symbols expressing some aspect of the archetype). The circle—whether a ball, a clock, a wheel, an egg, a hat, a flower, or a flying saucer; whether unbroken, broken, crossed, divided, spun about, and God knows what else—makes more than a cameo appearance in our explorations of symbolism. As a universal symbol, it's a major player.

ouroboros

✤ 4 ✤

THE TERRIBLE TWOS AND THE DYNAMIC DUOS: SYMBOLS OF THE CREATION

WHAT WOULD LIFE BE LIKE IF WE NEVER encountered any resistance? Imagine someone sleepwalking in an environment with no obstacles. What would make the person wake up?

What if we never heard the word *no*? What if life answered with an affirmative, accepting "Okay, yes!" to every response we made? Would we ever come to know that we exist? A strange question, but imagine . . . going through life without having to make any effort to assert oneself. Might we go through life like the snake biting its tail?

A baby feels hunger pains and cries, but the baby cannot feed itself. Time passes, someone/something happens, and pain goes away. How long and predictable between cry and response-lessening pain—such is the baby's world. Sometime later, inevitably, the parent must restrain the toddler from doing something it wants. The toddler begins to experience making some exertion against resistance. When the child inevitably begins to holler "No!" itself and rejects his or her parents' requests, the child is learning about what it means to be distinct from others. The child maybe got the idea from the parents when the child heard from them "No!" and was restrained in some way. The resistance the child encountered was functioning as a wakeup call. The child comes to practice it as a means of asserting his or her wakefulness.

There's that familiar saying that expresses the wisdom here: "To make an omelet, one has to crack the eggs." What was perfectly round was also uncreative, self-contained. The circle must be broken for creation to begin. How does it happen?

Meditation is a time-honored place to explore mysteries of consciousness. The instructions on how to meditate are simple: "Pay attention to the breathing. When awareness notices that the mind has wandered, bring the attention back to the breathing." Simple instructions, these are, for mindfulness meditation. What happens?

Follow the meditation instructions for a bit. Sooner or later we notice that we have become lost in thought. When did that happen? We can't recall. Most folks consider that moment a failure experience. Actually, however, it is a moment of success! Why? The intention for mindfulness just won out over the sleepwalking trance that was going on. That "coming out" of trance, "awakening" to "become aware," is the essential creation of self-aware consciousness that we're talking about here. What causes meditators to become aware that their mind has wandered?

Before that moment of inner realization, we have the symbol of the snake biting its tail. After that moment, we have the circle now somehow broken or divided into two. The universal sign for *No!* or *Don't!* is a bright red circle divided by a backward slash through it! A coincidence? No, no, no, it shakes its finger at us.

Here's another example of the divide-and-create theme from the story of Genesis in the Bible and how this symbolism plays out.

"Now the earth was unformed and void, and darkness was upon the face of the deep; and the spirit of God hovered over the face of the waters. And God said: 'Let there be light.' And there was light. And God saw the light, and that it was good; and God divided the light from the darkness."

Notice three things in this account.

First, God creates by separating, by dividing into two, light and dark, heaven and earth, male and female. Second, prior to the division, there was a void (the motif of the circle as empty). Third, the separation created judgment ("It was good").

Later in Genesis, the theme is repeated in what happens after Adam and Eve bite into the apple:

"And the eyes of them both were opened, and they knew that they were naked; and they sewed fig-leaves together."

Biting into the apple creates the consciousness of separation.

The united circle has been divided. By this symbolism, we come to understand that Paradise was an unconscious state of merger, or oneness. Prior to that bite, it seems Adam and Eve were sleep-walking through creation.

Here's an interesting little experiment to re-experience the moment of biting into the apple and the consequences.

Turn attention inward, toward the breathing, as in meditation. Just become aware of the breathing, noticing what occurs as breathing happens.

. . .

Having had a chance to observe the breathing, let's review what might have been experienced.

I have found that when folks receive the instructions to turn their attention toward their breathing, there seems to be a reflex, not just to look but to grab on as well, as if it were out of control and there was need to adjust it in some way. It's as if, when we turn our attention to our breathing, we have a "Look, nobody's got a hand on the steering wheel, better grab it!" type of reaction.

Shining the light upon the body's breathing typically rec-reates that moment of the dawning of awareness of an inner "I" separate from the rest of what we might experience. Before thinking to attend to our breathing, we weren't much aware of the breath. It was happening automatically, by instinct. We might say that we and our breath were one, or fused into a single being. By turning our attention toward our breathing, our relationship to it changed—now there were two, me and my breath. I experience myself as separate from my breath.

We've cut the circle in two, and that is the birth of consciousness, the dawning of "I am." We cut ourselves off from the paradise of unconscious breathing and enter the harsh new world in which breathing becomes our "job." We could choose to let go of that task, but that's a further development.

Free will comes with a price: having to make choices and decisions, separating the yes from the no. It's work.

Biting into the apple was a rupture of the perfect circle. The kids were kicked out of the Paradise Playground and forced to grow up by making some effort! And thus the journey begins. Much of symbolism is about the subsequent experiences that are likely encountered on that trip onward to conscious, cocreative oneness with the mysteries of life. It takes a lot of experience to learn how to go with the flow and have it take you to your destiny.

A parting question to get the dynamic duo symbol fermenting on the brain: Would creation exist if there was no awareness of it?

SOME SYMBOLS TO SAMPLE

Laughing until you
cry—why?

Heads and tails—
opposite but connected

No! Stop! How do you
feel now?

How can we mingle if
we're separate first?

SOME SYMBOLS TO SAMPLE

Opposites attract.

It takes two to tangle.

Take a bite.

Twin energies

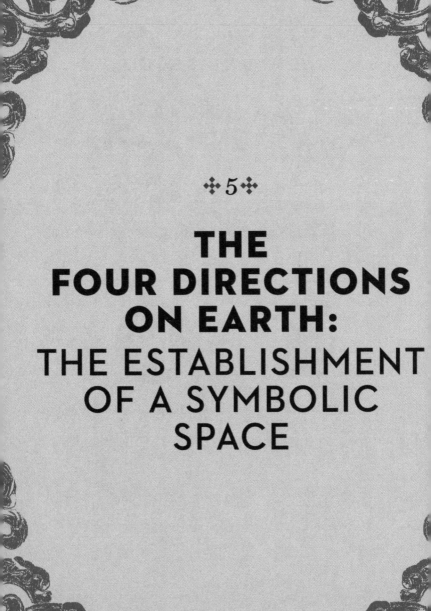

✤ 5 ✤

THE FOUR DIRECTIONS ON EARTH:

THE ESTABLISHMENT OF A SYMBOLIC SPACE

SYMBOLISM TELLS A STORY. IT'S A STORY OF THE human experience, of us becoming conscious and creation becoming conscious of itself through us. It is not the story told by bones, pottery shards, carbon dating, or electron analysis; nor is it the story of the changes in life-forms on the planet. Symbolism tells the story about something that is invisible to the eye, somewhat insubstantial yet available to our feeling within, or intuition. Symbolism tells the story about what it's like to become aware as a living being within a physical world.

We use feeling and imagination to empathize with symbols so that we may become aware of the stories symbols tell. What is it like to be suddenly born into awareness? What is it like to go from sleep to wakefulness?

Our brief experiment turning on awareness of breathing gives us a simple everyday example of what the symbols of duality suggest: Creating by dividing into two has implications and consequences. Waking up into being? What's the story on that?

Once we come into being, it's only natural to look around. Let's try it and see.

There's the world out there in front of us. Turn around. There's a world behind us. One arm points to the right, while the other arm points to the left. Duality repeats itself, both with forward and backward motion, and with right and left. In terms of directions on a map, there are four cardinal points. There are also topographical distances—an up and a down—that exist outside the confines of the printed page. These divisions occur frequently in the literature of human understanding. For example, in the biblical story of Eden, after the earth is separated from heaven, Eden is found to be the center of four converging rivers on Earth.

The circle divides into two. Each half divides again to form four segments. We're getting the Earth plane mapped out, structured by the compass points of north to south, and east to west. Life in the material realm seems to happen within a total and self-contained system that is continually cycling and recycling through the play of opposites. An opposing pair of opposite twins provides a foursome material space—a square dance!

Among the Lakota tribe of Native Americans, for example, the space in which life happens stretches out in four directions toward certain pillars, or stable qualities that support the possibilities for life to happen. In his book *Seven Arrows,* author Hyemeyohsts Storm explains this aspect of Native American spirituality. He points to north as the place of wisdom, west as the place of introspection, south as the place of innocence, and east as the place of illumination. Each corner has associated with it a color and an animal. In this worldview, the entire circle, or "sacred hoop," is a mirror of each of us individually, and also mirrors creation as a whole. Human development, according to this native spirituality, requires a trip around the circle to develop a balanced repertoire in all four quarters of existence.

The compass is a good image of the symbolism we have been exploring here. The magnetic pull of Earth gives the compass its standard north—an objective, material foundation to the intuitive impression of the "straight ahead" direction. From such an anchor, the other directions fall into place. As we look around the compass, opportunity is calling from all four directions. Whichever way we go, we are destined to meet ourselves. The cross, made by the twin polarities, and the opportunities they provide, will be cause for our later exploring "mandala" symbolism, whereby the circle is not divided by the cross but is fulfilled by it.

There is something about the four-sided square that suggests reliable integrity. The expression "fair and square" dates to a Masonic tradition related to building. Here we can trace a figure of speech referencing a particular symbol back to specific facts. The mystic mason intuited a connection between how God created the universe and how man should build his home. The square, a shape created by the relationship between lines creating a perfect ninety-degree angle, provided a matrix for building that had reliable and highly valuable qualities. We can build on it with the same degree of confidence with which God builds the world. Its four corners provide a space for exploration.

This world that we can now explore, what is it made of, what do we see? In the early Western tradition, the material world was made of the four elements: earth, air, fire, and water. The symbolism of the four directions as opportunities for experience now morph analogically to four qualities of the *substance* of experience. How might we explore inwardly the meaning of these very rudimentary symbols?

Becoming one with what we wish to be intuitive about seems to come naturally to children. Here is an exercise I like to do when I teach children: I ask the kids to put on a performance, suggesting, "Do a dance for us that will show us grown-ups how it feels for a raindrop to evaporate into a cloud." It's really fun to watch the kids perform this event from nature. They move about, using their faces, arms, and legs to suggest some process of dissolving, maybe floating, or even, by some of the peaceful expressions, slipping into some kind of comfortable restfulness. How do they do it? Ask the kids and they tell us right away: They pretend to be raindrops, and the rest is easy!

Imagine then the unfolding story of the birth of creation. Through its symbol-making process of communicating with itself, the creative imagination feels a circle opening into the dance of two. The dynamic, creative tension in this dance awakens the presence of awareness itself, and the world comes into conscious being. Everything that happens afterward is under constant surveillance. This new awareness discovers the light it shines in four directions. This new awareness encounters experiences of four different substances of material being. With so many factors at play, the story can now branch out in many directions and support the actions of many players in the dance of life.

SOME SYMBOLS TO SAMPLE

When you know where
North is, you . . .

Right in the crosshairs

Right here!

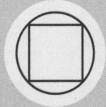

Four square is right on . . .

SOME SYMBOLS TO SAMPLE

Out of the Earth

What gets you fired up?

Full of air . . .

You are all wet!

✦ 6 ✦

THE BODY IS THE TEMPLE: SYMBOLS OF OUR EARTHLY INHABITATION

I AM SMOKING A CIGARETTE IN CHURCH. THE CONgregants stare at me in silent disbelief. I begin to feel a bit awkward if not downright guilty.

When I wake up from this dream, it's obvious to me that my tobacco habit is on my mind. Why am I smoking in church? Is tobacco my religion? Everybody is upset about what I'm doing. It's polluting the church. Then it hits me: The body is the *temple*.

The dream came at a time when I was beginning my first spiritual study group. The symbolization of the body as "church" introduces a spiritual theme to the contemplation of the physical body. It brings the issue of the tobacco habit into the spiritual realm while at the same time anchoring the concern in the body itself. Here we see again the symbol functioning as more than simply a coded sign. Instead, the church symbol is evocative, bringing various areas of meaning to me as I think about my daytime motivation to be "spiritual" by joining this group. Yet here I am, at the same time, polluting the church. The symbol operates actively to break down compartmentalization and the denial it enables.

The symbolization of the body as a temple dates back at least to the Old Testament. As evidence that God can visit the body-church and reverse diseases in that body, we present to you Asclepius, the Greek god of medicine. Stone tablets exist testifying to miraculous healings occurring during the night among those sleeping in the temples of Asclepius, such as at Epidaurus. The recorded healings, although directed at physical disease, seem symbolic or dreamlike in nature. One ancient inscribed testimony describes that while the petitioner slept in Asclepius's temple, he was bitten by a snake and awakened healed from a cancerous sore.

By the time of Socrates, the dream "incubation" miracles of Asclepius were already enshrined in sculptures as objects for prayer. We can learn something of our body-dwelling from the symbols from that time, of Asclepius's wooden staff and the encircling snake, which is active today to indicate healing and medicine. In that sense, the image has become a code, yet the symbols speak of a mystery yet to be fully realized.

Let's place the symbols of Asclepius on our brain and see what happens. The staff is of wood and, thus, from a tree. The tree and the snake have in common that they shed their skin and renew themselves every year. Yet they are of different natures, one a plant, the other an animal. Is there some yin and yang creative duality going on here? The staff has been shaped by a human hand, while the serpent remains untamed and still alive. Could it be that by combining these two realities, something new, as in healing, might occur? Why do we need healing medicine in the first place? Is it something to do with being human and which the balance of instinctual nature might cure?

As long as we wonder with the symbol and don't conclude about it, we still have the symbol on the brain. Try to formulate a final answer, and what we get is the end of the symbolization process and the beginning of having ideas in hand—ideas that, at best, might stimulate some further research or experimentation.

Dreams are notorious for revealing things unseen. In the case of the body and its activities, Aristotle wrote about how subtle bodily sensations are easy to ignore during the busyness of the day. As we are relatively quiet and inactive in sleep, those same bodily sensations have an easier time of being noticed. The common analogy is that the stars are always there but are easier to see once the sun goes down.

The implication was that some dreams might be early-warning signals of impending disease. From that idea grew the idea that dreams were by nature prophetic in many ways. That idea gave birth to the first dream dictionary, the *Oneirocritica*, compiled by the Greek Artemidorus in the second century CE and still published and available today. In it, dream symbols are *equated* with future events. It has inspired many imitators and successors, and such dream prophecy books use this exact same approach as guides to the future. Their "*this* means *that*" divinatory code pattern gave symbol dictionaries a bad reputation among those wishing to evolve greater consciousness from meditating on symbolism.

Research in authoritative, historical sources (of which there are many available today on the Internet) concerning symbols regarding the body will reveal how the body has been symbolized for millennia as a *dwelling*. The form that dwelling takes, and the details, evolve with history and the artifacts in a person's environment. Several millennia in the past, a person suffering from congestion might have a dream in which their hut needed sweeping. Today, that person would dream about a house in need of vacuuming. In each case, the symbolization function of the mind turns to its experience in the daily dwelling place for analogies to express an event happening in the body.

In modern times, aspects of a house come into play as raw material to symbolize bodily events. Plumbing and electrical references are obvious candidates. Clogs, leaks, disconnections, swellings, fires, rotting, and all such things seen in one's outer physical habitation can become enlisted as symbols to suggest subtle events going on within. An electrical fire in a dream, for example, with dramatic sparks and horrible sounds, is how symbolism can add a motivational element to perhaps stimulate some action on the facts it suggests.

In today's moving world, people spend enough time in their automobiles that the dream's symbolizing function might represent the body as the person's *vehicle*. Is it handling okay? Is it having trouble making it up the hills? Is the carburetor working okay?

For the most part, however, the home base, with its windows, doors, floors, rooms, stairs, etc., readily symbolizes the body and its events. It's easy, I believe, to intuit the "fit," and how using a dwelling-type symbol for the body can be quite expressive of the nuances of the experience of being "a spirit dwelling in a physical home."

SOME SYMBOLS TO SAMPLE

Any body home?

A dwelling place for
the divine

Asclepius: a healer in
your dreams

Something material with
something spiritual

SOME SYMBOLS TO SAMPLE

Home shoe home

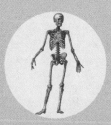

The bare bones, but nobody is home

The vehicle for your adventures

Which form do you inhabit?

THE TREES, RIVERS, AND MOUNTAINS:
SYMBOLS OF OUR INNER NATURE

AS PART OF OUR ESTRANGEMENT FROM EDEN, we experience nature as external and separate from ourselves. We are, nevertheless, an integral part of nature, and we cannot help but express its truths. Our bodies are made of earth. Our biological being is part of the web of life. It should be no surprise, then, that humans have perceived objects from nature to symbolize aspects of the human experience on the planet. Many of the oldest civilizations valued the close observation of nature as the key to wisdom.

We and nature are one, and we can find in every item in nature a sacred mirror in which we may see aspects of ourselves. We can begin with the fundamental building blocks of nature, such as the four elements: earth, air, fire, and water. Taking a lesson from the children's dance of the evaporating raindrops, we can use our body to take us into our imagination, and within it is our ability to unite with any and all our relations in nature. Such practices can feel like a reunion.

As an example, let's take water. A common definition is that it refers to the origin of life in the ocean and our origin in the womb. Dark and foreboding, the ocean depths remind us of all we do not know. Let's explore it with the light of our imagination. Let's create water dances. Imagine being water flowing in a river, and move like it. Imagine being water as big and deep as the ocean, and move like it. Imagine water falling as drops from the sky—what's the ride like? Does water feel wet to itself? Slippery? Can water be happy? Can it be angry? What aspects of ourselves can we recognize as we imagine being water in its various expressions?

Carl Jung, the turn-of-the-century psychiatrist who uncovered the kind of evidence to make the study of symbolism most productive, proposed that the four elements may be analogous to frames of mind. Like opposing directions on a compass, he envisioned them as pairs of opposing mental functions: perceiving versus judging on the one hand, and looking inward versus looking outward on the other. He further refined these pairs as thinking versus feeling—the judging functions—and intuition versus sensation—the perceiving functions. In this way, the aspects of the world that are available to us, that we can become aware of and have a relationship to, depend upon the method or means—the frame of mind—by which we approach them.

Take Earth, for example. What does it mean to be "grounded"? Imagine being Earth, solid and heavy. What do those experiences have to do with being attentive to the senses or to being perceptive? Simultaneously exploring these differing dimensions of the symbol takes us deeper into the consciousness that symbol evokes.

Nature inspires. History documents that fact. We ourselves can affirm the rapture nature creates. It inspires because it draws us in. Somehow we participate in nature. We have an aesthetic relationship with nature; we imagine being in it, of it. Scientific studies have confirmed that nature excites our imagination. Being able to see nature out a window makes us feel better.

Our brain on nature is very similar to our brain on symbols. We are transported, moved, taken to places within, as symbolism stimulates the imagination.

Stories of adventure take place in an environment of nature, with mountains to climb, caves for shelter, rivers for travel, and many vistas for view. All these natural environments suggest, symbolically, aspects of our experience moving through life, with its obstacles, opportunities, and moods. So many folks have had recurrent dreams of moving in a certain natural environment with a particular view or vista, pregnant with meaning.

Imagine how standing on the edge of a deep, dark forest is both inviting and intimidating at the same time. Moving into the unknown has many aspects and qualities.

Imagine standing on top of a mountain. What is it like to be so high up there, closer to the sky? The gods that resided on Mount Olympus in ancient Greece are now scattered among several cloud-covered peaks, inviting folks to risk their lives to become one with such a heightened consciousness. If we can begin to feel the pull of a lofty mountaintop, we are engaging the symbolism of the mountain.

Where are you at? What kind of space are you in? These colloquialisms for inquiring about a person's state of mind both use suggestive environmental symbolism in forming the question.

Symbols from nature can help us resolve dilemmas that are otherwise difficult to think through. As a case in point, how do we decide how much of ourselves we can give to others, and what do we need to keep for ourselves? It's a very difficult dilemma to resolve. Consider moving the dilemma to the symbol of a tree. As a tree, my purpose is to grow fruits to share, which will also spread my seeds. I want people to eat my fruit. But please, do not tear off my leaves, as I need them to grow my food. Please do not molest my blossoms, as they are in the early stages of my gifts. But please *do eat of my fruits* and share them with others.

Here's a simple crafts project that is a fun way to create symbolic self-portraits of our personal qualities. Take a walk in nature with a meditative intention. Expect to be "greeted" by various elements in nature. Assume the element is mirroring a personal quality. Dialogue with the nature object to discover the meaning or connection. Collect permitted souvenirs of these encounters and arrange them into a design to suggest important attributes of creation. Meditate on this nature collage as if to realize, "This is me!" Pay attention to the thoughts, daydreams, and memories that pass by during the meditation, as such notions may bring important insights.

SOME SYMBOLS TO SAMPLE

Behind the clouds

You are growing
like a tree!

When it rains, it . . .

Which do you prefer?
The rainbow or the
clouds?

SOME SYMBOLS TO SAMPLE

Someone is beginning
to flower.

Keep on keeping on—
you'll get there!

Just around the bend

Good to the last drop

✜ 8 ✜

FOLLOWING TURTLE WAITING ON BEAR: ANIMAL SYMBOLISM AND OUR NATIVE INSTINCTS

W E'VE SHARED THIS PLANET WITH ANIMALS since time began. We've learned a lot from watching them and having relationships with them. Just as with the elements from nature, we see ourselves in the animals. They can have tremendous symbolic value for us. We identify with animals, project ourselves imaginatively onto the animals, and daydream about what it must be like to be such an animal. When animals serve a symbolic function, we can explore their qualities and benefit from the "symbol-on-the-brain" process. Sensitizing and expanding our consciousness to potentialities within us and how to best relate to them is one of the gifts animals offer.

We can ask ourselves, "What animal sparks my imagination? If I could be any animal, which one? Has an animal appeared synchronistically in my life from time to time?" Such questions can take us into our symbolic mind-set, so that we can learn from the animals.

A turtle has been one of my teachers. As a child I would often come across a turtle, and I'd try to make a pet of it. It would invariably escape and disappear. As a first-year psychology graduate student, I obtained a desert tortoise and attempted to train it to come when I called. Fresh lettuce or a strawberry was the reward. The signal was my speaking its name, Dr. Boring, honoring a famous historian of psychology, Dr. Edwin Boring. After much trial and error, I learned that the turtle could hear my voice best when I used a very low vibrato tone. As I tell the story now to kids at summer camp, the turtle taught this psychologist how to chant! Actually, the turtle has taught me more than that.

Slower than a rabbit but more reliable, the turtle carries its home with it and sticks its neck out with reluctance and great care. The turtle shell is shaped and marked like the planet Earth. Ancient Hindu mythology has the world supported by a turtle. Native Americans refer to their homeland as "Turtle Island." Using these characteristics as a guide, we might express turtle wisdom as, "Life is long; let's slow down, take the time to experience all there is, and move out in harmony with life. We can't separate ourselves from our earthly home."

As I researched and contemplated the literature on turtle symbolism, I became more mindful of my habits with regard to turtles. I stopped wanting to own one as a captured pet. I became more fascinated by the mantra, "In patience you possess your soul." This biblical quote is a good example of what Native Americans might refer to as "turtle medicine."

Native American teachings emphasize the spiritual or symbolic value of animals. In their view of the web of life, each animal has a function to fulfill by playing a role that takes advantage of the animal's special attributes. Thus each animal possesses its own unique "medicine" or wisdom. Of all the animals, perhaps it is the bear that they hold in highest regard. Some say it is because when the bear stands erect, it looks humanlike. Animal/human—here is a contrast/duality that adds power to the symbol.

We are familiar with Smokey Bear, the bear market, the ubiquitous teddy bear, the Alaska governess's term for herself—Mama Grizzly—and the bears that appear on the flags of Russia and California.

Bears make news, especially when they leave their wilderness habitat and visit human places. There's a lot of damage, for sure. On the other hand, there's a certain amusement, spectator value, and a lot of support for the bears. The official response seems to be, "Don't tempt the bears, or else we'll have to kill them as they become dangerous nuisances."

That bears stimulate ambivalence is a key to getting bear symbolism going on the brain. I can easily imagine dancing with a bear, but then I can also see it suddenly turning on me. I feel the power of a mother, both to nurture with love and even to wound me as a way of protecting me from greater trauma.

In a dream, a mama bear chases me up a tree. What do I do now? I read that mama bear teaches her young to climb a tree at her signal of danger and not to come down before permission is given, or she smacks them. When the time comes for the cubs to be on their own, she sends them up a tree, but then she wanders off, never to return. After enough time passes, the bear cubs finally come down the tree, and by breaking mama's fierce rule, they earn their independence, sad as it might feel at first.

In a dream years later, soon after seeing an actual bear climb a tree in my yard, I am walking along with a bear, keeping company together. In dealing with adversity or challenges, I had learned the art of hibernation, the simple act of taking a nap to awaken with a refreshed perspective. I've learned from bear "medicine" how solitude is important to my creative process. On the other hand, I've had to learn how to recognize when I'm being protective of one of my creations (including my ego) when I start to get angry—"Okay, mama bear, calm down, and let's see if I can handle it. I know I have your strength going for me."

Following the path of a couple of animals is a good way to explore symbolism and what it has to offer. Whether the attraction or curiosity about an animal stems from a special encounter or not, there is much to be gained by reading up on the animal: What are its habits? What does it contribute to the web of life? Integrating this kind of important information with some experiments in aligning with that animal's spirit is a good plan. Imagine being that animal. Ask questions like, "What does it do for fun? How can I have fun in a similar fashion? Can I participate in the animal's contribution to the web of life?" If I can think of some action I can take on behalf of that animal's welfare, I believe that such actions, conducted ritually with the intent of evolving my conscious understanding of the meaning of that animal and the role of its medicine in my life, will prove rewarding.

SOME SYMBOLS TO SAMPLE

You may admire me.

I'm back!

Slow and steady

Can you bear it?

SOME SYMBOLS TO SAMPLE

Horsing around

Don't give us false warnings.

Nobody can run like me.

I'm just curious.

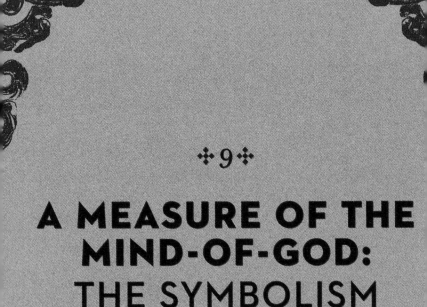

✛ 9 ✛

A MEASURE OF THE MIND-OF-GOD: THE SYMBOLISM OF NUMBERS

HOW COULD SOMETHING SO PRECISE AS NUMbers have the kind of suggestive or evocative qualities needed to drive the symbolic process? Two plus two equals four, and four equals four, nothing more, nothing less. *Equals* and *symbolizes* imply very different correspondences, as we know. It doesn't seem possible that such abstract things like numbers could have proven symbolic significance. But they do!

What about having a lucky number? What makes it special? What does thinking about that number bring to mind? Answering such questions is a good review lesson concerning how symbolism works its charms.

I first entered into the realm of number symbolism in fourth grade. We were working on learning our multiplication tables. I had to memorize a lot. To simplify my task, I visualized arrangements of marbles, the coin of my realm at that time. To visualize two times two, which equals four, I would see a square of marbles, arranged two by two. As I learned how to find what little numbers make up big numbers, I found the marble approach helpful.

There are so many possibilities. As always, the properties of something are the source of its symbolic energy. Explore the properties of numbers that allow them to be arranged in various patterns. It can be very entertaining, with perhaps the symbolism process working in the faraway background, to arrange large numbers of marbles into different patterns.

Another way of getting into the symbolism of numbers is by thinking about how we learned to count. Experts believe that numbers began by counting things on our fingers, giving the number ten its importance. Our standard arithmetic, and the way we write it out, is based upon ten and its square, one hundred, then one thousand, etc.

Add the toes to the fingers, and we get twenty. The Mayans used this *vigesimal*, or base twenty, system in their astronomical calculations to become more accurate in heavenly calculations than the earlier Mesopotamians.

The Mesopotamians favored the number sixty as a basis for counting. This decision comes from their counting the days in an annual seasonal cycle (they counted 360, off by a bit more than five days). Also, using a compass to draw a circle, that same compass setting will walk around the circle's circumference in six steps. These six points define a hexagon created by six triangles.

Triangles are crucial to construction. The number three is the smallest number that allows for creating a boundary and enclosing some space. As carpenters know, the triangle is the most simple and stable of the forms in construction. No wonder that they say, "Three times a charm," although that might not be the original reason for saying it. Yet, in so many stories, having to do something three times, or if something happens three times, makes it real, or committed, solid, true.

Being "true" can also be a term referring to the number four, as implied in the "four corners" of Earth, or "four directions." The Masons established their ideals based on their being "on the level." Being square with level makes something plumb upright and predictable. No matter where along the construction we might go, everything remains in square relationship to each other.

Pythagoras was the ancient Greek genius who figured out the length of the shortcut between opposite corners of a square (and thus finding a relationship between the square and the triangle). He then devised an entire religion out of what he and his students discovered about the properties of numbers. He discovered how those properties are mirrored in what we hear as music—the musical scale. Today the study of "sacred geometry" finds many correspondences between the mathematics of music and the geometry of the objects in creation.

The numbers one, four, seven, and twelve are the most frequent stars of the number family when it comes to spiritual or metaphysical traditions. Researching the history of the symbolization of these numbers finds that looking skyward, toward the gods, stars, planets, and moon, has played a significant role in the reputation of these numbers. There are the twelve signs of the zodiac, for example, giving us the twelve months of the year. There are four phases of the moon, each seven days long. The cycles of life, in its various manifestations, become yet another mode of expression that nature uses to suggest its secrets.

The number 147 is constructed of three multiplied by seven multiplied by seven. [On the other hand, if you were to look at it as 1+4+7, then it would give you 12, another special number, and then, 1+2 would be 3.] Suddenly, the number 147 is full of surprises. This latter procedure is that of numerology, a unique system of working with numbers symbolically. In that divinatory discipline, any number, regardless of size, can be equated to one of the nine single digits by adding up the digits comprising that number until a single digit results. Each digit has a particular symbolic domain within a framework of a complete digital cycle.

Should a person become stalked by a particular number appearing repeatedly, perhaps almost magically, then certain strategies might apply. First, the number may be a prod from memory, associated with a past incident wishing to be used to understand something in the present. Second, the source of the attraction or curiosity may be explored in the numerical constituents of the number, as in the different numerical patterns it's possible to make from that many marbles. Third, the digits used to signify the number may be combined to result in a final single digit for numerological interpretation.

Meditating on the number and looking for it to appear in a dream, or in daily life, may provide a context that would reflect some added meaning. Using the number as a basis for an arts or crafts project offers interesting possibilities. Preparing a little "offering" for the spirit of a symbol can result in an increased sense of relationship with that symbol. Flatter the gods that rule that number and its relatives, and your efforts to understand a particular number might receive a special blessing.

SOME SYMBOLS TO SAMPLE

Triangles get tight.

Elemental

I could count on
one hand.

It's as easy as . . .

SOME SYMBOLS TO SAMPLE

Count your beads.

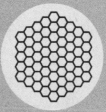

Often seen in nature

They either are, or
they're not.

Shadow and light

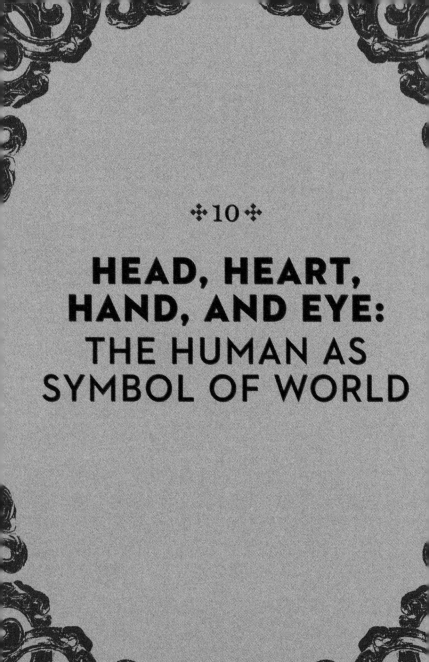

✤ 10 ✤

HEAD, HEART, HAND, AND EYE:
THE HUMAN AS SYMBOL OF WORLD

THE ENTIRE WORLD, INCLUDING THE HUMAN beings in it, is a creation born from images in the mind of the Creator, Mind-of-God. This idea is another one of the Hermetic principles mentioned in *The Kybalion*. Everything bears the "maker's mark." As a mirror of the Creator, the world is quite immense. On the other hand, the human being provides a perfect mirror. As the Bible expresses the Hermetic principle of correspondence, "God created man in His own image." The study of the human would reveal truths about the universe and its Creator.

Imagine, then, a human being standing up, legs spread, feet firmly planted, arms raised from the side. Make a few leaps of thought. What experience within suggests something about the world "out there"? How is the human a mirror of creation?

There's a feeling of aliveness inside, for example, that renders the aliveness outside quite apparent. What makes for the sense of aliveness we feel inside ourselves? The awareness of movement, breathing. Something or someone is initiating movement, and that makes for life. It is easy to feel one's way into the idea of the breath being a reflection of the wind, an animating spirit. Breathing it all in creates a sense of oneness, of participation in the creative force of life.

What else can we feel inside? We can sense our pulse, the heat of the blood, the heart being the central furnace and pump of this energy. It is just like the sun, then, that shines its heat down upon us. This heat is some kind of fuel source, just as the sun is. The heart is in the center of the body, joins Heaven and Earth, and thus exists as the center of the cross.

One of the symbolic dimensions of the Aztec-Mayan religious life was the worship of the sun and its feeding through the sacrifice of the heart. The energy of the heart was sacrificed to feed the sun. The meeting of heart and sun occurred at the center of the cross formed by the pyramid's floor plan at every level, up to the very top, closest to heaven. The intersection of Heaven and Earth occurred there as an energy exchange between heart and sun.

One of the ironies of history is imagined in Spanish author Salvador de Madariaga's beautiful novel *The Heart of Jade*. When Spanish conquistador Hernán Cortés met with Aztec emperor Montezuma in Mexico, they both saw crosses and hearts in one another's insignias and displays. Although the Spaniards wished to annihilate the heathens, they were unaware of how much pagan heritage they as Christians had themselves. The symbolism in the

Christian insignia expressed intuitive feelings of love and faith that were also present in the worldview of the ancient Mexicans they were destroying.

Part of the heart's symbolic power is how it can bring together opposites. Not just linking Heaven and Earth, spirit and matter, Christians and pagans, but also love and hate, joy and sorrow, near and far. Consider the image found on cigar box labels as well as spiritual objects of Jesus with His heart exposed, dripping with blood yet sprouting flowers or flames from the wound. Can there be life-giving creativity in suffering?

While the sun and the wind are essential to life, as are the heart and lungs, it is the pattern of relationships among the elements of creation that forms creation. Shake hands with the world. We use our hands to touch, to handle, to communicate, to make signs, and to hurt others. We use our hands perhaps more than any other part of the body, and so they have more symbolic functions than other body parts. Prehistoric cave paintings testify to the popularity of the handprint signature.

One of the more common hand symbols is the *hamsa*, which is an image of the right hand, open and upside down, as if it were a hand from above. Thus it symbolizes such suggestive themes as protection, good luck, being chosen, etc. Hands are something we have two of, as we have two arms, two legs, two feet, two eyes, and two ears. One can be dominant over the other, and in life sometimes we have to allow the other to have expression. We notice that there's a right-handed way and a left-handed way, and we can also find balance between our hands. Many hand gestures are expressing symbolically, suggestive of certain experiences.

I can ask myself, "When something happens to me, how do I usually handle it? Do I feel I had a hand in it? Do I keep my hands behind my back or do I take a hands-on approach? On the other hand, how do I like to be handled myself?"

Sometimes the hand has an eye in it, which adds an extra element of drama. Add an eye and we have a particularly watchful guide and protector. On the other hand, an all-seeing eye can evoke a bit of concern, of paranoia, about the "evil eye."

An interesting thought experiment is to imagine a special video camera recording our every moment, including both our internal experiences and external actions. Most folks are uncomfortable with such a prospect. Upon reflection, the source of the discomfort has to do with self-judgment. Recall the story of the apple bite in Eden, which had the psychedelic effect of thrusting Adam and Eve into awareness of self as distinct from other, the separation that we call self-consciousness. With separation comes the knowledge of good and evil—in other words, judgment.

Thus the all-seeing eye becomes a mirror—am I accepting or judging? The eye in the pyramid on the back of the dollar suggests an awareness that has been a constant witness to the development and products of humanity. Is it a silent witness or a judge?

A cartoon rendering of planet Earth with a face on it gives the impression of the planet as a living being. In Villa Hermosa, Mexico, there are giant heads sitting on the ground. These ancient Olmec sculptures appear as if emerging from Earth. Later expression of this same theme has the head of the Mayan god Kukulkan ("Feathered Serpent") emerging from the mouth of the snake. In each case, the head is suggestive of consciousness, as if being evolved and born out of the unconscious Earth. We might also interpret them as suggesting that the world was sprouting consciousness in the form of humans.

SOME SYMBOLS TO SAMPLE

We can see it in your hand.

I'm getting a head of myself.

Kukulkan

Don't put it in your mouth.

SOME SYMBOLS TO SAMPLE

I gotta hand it to you.

To know in your heart

Love spoken here

Protected from evil

✣11✣

THE EVOLUTION OF ENLIGHTENMENT: SYMBOLS FROM SPIRITUAL TRADITIONS

SPIRITUALITY CONCERNS THE EXPANSION OF consciousness, from local to universal, and the typical transformations or stages of development in that growth toward a life of conscious interrelationships. Mythologies, stories constructed from symbols, describe the spiritual path as one of awakening and a transformation from darkness and illusion to one of light and conscious harmony with creation.

The senses are perfect for interacting with the material world. As long as "nobody's home," the transformation of energy moving through the *ouroboric* cycle of physical life is sufficient unto itself. What happens when something "wakes up" and finds itself as a living spirit embedded in this ongoing physical creation? What's next? How do we deal with the contradictions of being a free spirit trapped in a physical body?

The award of being the designated "oldest known

human-made symbol" goes to one with a tainted reputation. The oldest known symbol, etched in stone, shrouded in mystery, suggestive to the imagination, is the swastika.

Scientists do not know how far back in history the image goes or toward what idea or realization those swastikas were symbolizing—certainly not the idea of a political party or nation state! The image emerged in a prehistoric period and spread most everywhere.

The swastika is a riff on the symbol of the cross as earthly compass and suggests the circle in which the cross is contained. Each end of the cross is bent or turned, traditionally toward the right, or clockwise. The cross begins to move, to circulate. Into the four directions of space there arises movement, circulation. It's easy to empathize with the image and feel movement within, excitement.

The urge, notion, or realization prompting the creation of swastikas evolved with time into expressions that provided more clues about the meaningful force behind the image. One of my favorites comes from the iconography of the ancient Maya and Aztec peoples, whose many variations on the simple swastika form suggest more of its nuanced intent.

The glyphs most swastika-like in these cultures are those identified as specifying the Aztec god Ollin Tonatiuh, translated from the Nahuatl language as "movement of the sun." Movement suggests getting things going—animation. How does this happen? One of the interesting things is that their glyphs for Ollin, when simplified, reveal a pattern very similar to the yin and yang symbol.

Movement happens by, or is equivalent to, the splitting of one into two opposing but complementary parts. It seems to be portraying the notion that God is vibration! Hermes Trismegistus, for example, declared as a basic principle that all is vibration. Edgar Cayce, an American mystic and psychic, described God as being of two complementary but opposite qualities: impersonal and physical, as in lightning; and personal and spiritual, as in the experience of "I am." If God is Love, then perhaps the pair of complementary and opposite experiences making up the "love vibration" might be "I am you" versus "I am not you."

The yin and yang has within it also the notion of each of the opposing pairs transforming into their partner: There is a dot of white in the largest black area, and a dot of black in the largest white area. So the opposition is not really opposing, but taking turns; it is cyclical and, thus, one. Here the symbol is giving us more informational details about the divisive split needed for creativity. Although the sound of *No!* can seem quite destructive, the yin and yang symbol suggests that it will turn into a *Yes!* later on, so that the estrangement or separation is really illusory. The notion of movement also hints at the later realization by Albert Einstein of the "relativity" that exists between time and space.

The oneness in the play of opposites receives special

symbolization in the image of the mirror. Looking into the mirror, will we fall in love with that person in the mirror, as Narcissus did, or will we recognize the image as being a reflection of ourselves? Or is there yet another secret here?

In the Shinto religion indigenous to Japan, for example, a mirror is placed in the temple in the same way a Christian church would place a cross: as a focal point in front of the adherents who have gathered to worship. The cross brings two opposites together, man and God, nature and spirit. How then might a mirror do the same thing? The student who is ready will ask, "How can mirroring oneself to oneself reveal the God within?" The answer also lies within.

If the simple creative principle of the dance of opposites receives any further amplification, it comes from the Hermetic principle "the Many are One." In this case, the principle suggests that the many parts of creation are actually a unity, and each part is holographically reflecting the whole. Imagine a leaf from a tree: The veins in the leaf give the impression of a tree!

As a symbol of how All are One, I believe the best example is that of the World Tree, a pervasive motif that occurs throughout many cultures. One of my favorite expressions of this symbol is the Norse version, the Yggdrasil. We see the levels of the tree above and below ground—the circle of life is contained in a spherical display of expression. A remarkably similar expression from another culture is the Mayan tree of life.

An interesting project in personal symbolism is to create your own tree of life. Imagine being a mirror of creation as a model for the world tree. Imagine an animal, often a reptile, that's closest to the earth, like a snake or turtle. Choose a bird for the top of the head to communicate with heaven. On the left side, place something of the female principle. On the right, put something of the male. There would be at least seven branches of the tree, perhaps in pairs. The pairs might represent polar opposites in the expression of that branch. Imagine, the Many are One, and a personal mirror as well!

SOME SYMBOLS TO SAMPLE

There's as much
underground as above.

What is in heaven?

What goes around
comes around.

Now things are
beginning to move.

SOME SYMBOLS TO SAMPLE

Mirror, mirror on
the wall . . .

What is above is also below.

To see yourself as
others see you

Mirror in the temple

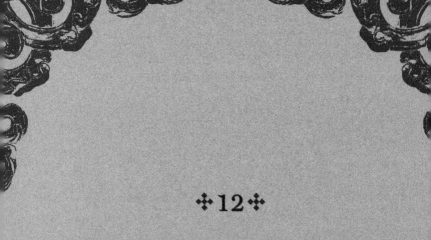

✛ 12 ✛

THE SUN'S TAIL WAGS THE WIND: SYMBOLS AND OBJECTIVE REALITY

T HERE IS WISDOM AT WORK IN THE CREATION of symbols. It seems to be a wisdom that wishes to convey itself, to become known as the source of the symbols—a wise source seeking recognition. Such was the conclusion of that influential Swiss psychiatrist Carl Jung. In his autobiography, *Memories, Dreams, Reflections*, he tells many fascinating stories from his life's work to help us gain a sense of some very challenging ideas.

Dr. Jung's own mysterious dreams, from childhood on, prodded him to wonder about the source of such bizarre ideas and images. Scholarly studies of mythology and ancient texts presented the good doctor with the same question—what was the source of the ideas in these stories? He also recognized similar themes in his patients' dreams, hallucinations, and artwork. These so-called subjective expressions appeared to Jung's seasoned mind as symbolic statements regarding the person's spiritual predicament. Rather than see the patient's symptomatology as a derangement of the mind, Jung saw it as an opening of the mind. A crisis created an opportunity in which a larger intelligence might speak—symbolically. Heeding the message brought about healing.

Symbolism was a key factor in Jung's discoveries. The controversial story of the "Solar Phallus Man," is perhaps the most dramatic example. Dr. Jung described it as important evidence for the existence of universal memory, or the collective unconscious. As Dr. Jung tells the story, he was just beginning his clinical practice, working at a hospital in Zürich, Switzerland. He confronted a wide range of patients, but there was one in particular who made quite an impression. It was someone who had a special "vision" to share. This was a man whose appearance and demeanor would not suggest anything exceptional, but nevertheless he had something very special he wanted folks to see. He was grabbing Dr. Jung by the collar and pointing at the window. "Look! Can you see it?!" the man insisted.

Dr. Jung looked out at the sky while the man described a long tail-like penis descending from the sun, waving back and forth. He asked Dr. Jung to move his head back and forth so he could see this tail and watch it move. The man explained that by wagging its tail, the sun was creating the wind. Dr. Jung didn't know what to think at the time, not being able to see the tail himself. He remained suspicious that there was something behind such a vision. It was years later before he got his answer.

The patient was, by then, deceased, and Jung was fully immersed in his scholarly research developing his theory of the collective unconscious and the archetypal nature of symbolism. Jung came across something newly translated, previously unknown to him. It was an ancient document about an initiation rite in a cult of Roman times. It described how the initiate, by moving his head from side to side, would see the sun's phallus waving back and forth, creating the wind. Jung immediately remembered his patient back at the Zürich hospital who had insisted, *insisted*, that he look at the sky.

The content of the patient's vision could not have come from something he had seen, heard of, or read about. No such accessible information was available. It had to come from within, from a universal memory, or collective unconscious. Dr. Jung later found further evidence for the more universal existence of this sun-tail theme. It was in an obscure Christian text describing a tube coming down from the sun to disappear under the dress of the Virgin Mother, showing how she was impregnated by the Holy Spirit.

At first Dr. Jung looked at the symbolism emerging from this supposed collective unconscious as being primarily a far-memory phenomenon. Over time, however, he realized there was a creative aspect at work in the unconscious mind of humanity. So he later called his discovery the "Objective Psyche." Today we'd call this same idea the "transpersonal mind," or "Mind at Large." Such terms represent the premise that the mind exists, on its own, without a brain to generate it. We do not "have a mind" of our own; instead we are embedded in

Mind at Large, and it has us in the grip of its dynamic structure. It's hard to imagine, but Einstein discovered and proved that space is not empty. Space is a force field that affects the physical realm. Similarly, the mind has its own prior and independent existence, and it shapes how we experience what we think of as reality. Over time, Dr. Jung's research led him to propose that there is a story brewing within a universal mind. One aspect of this story concerns the evolution of consciousness and our individual relationship to the whole. Another concerns living in the relationship between matter and meaning, or nature and spirit.

In the case of the "Solar Phallus Man" story, we can see such a relationship in the discovery, through our space probes, of solar wind. It was about a year after Dr. Jung's death that news began to arrive from the Mariner spacecraft about the steady flow of energy particles streaming off the sun in waves. As more data was collected, this same solar wind became the prime suspect in explaining why comets' tails point away from the sun and appear to wave in that "wind." Both the ancient initiation rite and the patient's hallucination pointed to something that was physically real. As the voice of the Objective Psyche, whether expressed in a vision, an hallucination, a religious ritual, or art, the symbolism reflects truths of experience, encountered both inwardly and externally.

Having the same source within the Mind-of-God, physical nature, and spiritual meaning mirror one another. The link appears in moments of meaningful coincidence. Dr. Jung created the term *synchronicity* to refer to this principle. It doesn't operate on the basis of a chain of cause-and-effect events, but rather through the coexistence of significantly meaningful events. Symbolism is the language that connects the inner and outer to make the meaningful connection. Following such connections is a form of research for enlightenment in its own right, as we'll see.

SOME SYMBOLS TO SAMPLE

Solar activity affects
life on Earth.

Atomic activity
mirrors the planets.

Is the sun the center
of it all?

The sun is the center
of our lives.

SOME SYMBOLS TO SAMPLE

The holy mother

Where do ideas
come from?

An omen of things
to come

She who makes it
happen

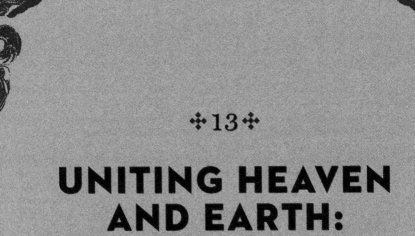

✦ 13 ✦

UNITING HEAVEN AND EARTH:
SUN DANCE SYMBOLISM AND PHOTOSYNTHESIS

FOLLOWING SYMBOLS TO SEE WHERE THEY MIGHT lead can bring about surprising and meaningful results. I'll share here one of my special stories that involves the dynamic relationship among various symbols, both in the realm of the mind and in the physical world. There's often more meaning to a symbol than we might imagine. It's a story that proves the mantra of symbolism: "As above, so below."

It began with a dream. It was the first night I spent in Virginia Beach, Virginia. I was staying as a guest at the home of Charles Thomas Cayce. The grandson of Edgar Cayce, the "Sleeping Prophet" who founded the Association for Research and Enlightenment, had invited me to the oceanfront town of its headquarters. Here's the dream.

We are gathered together in front of the headquarters of the Association for Research and Enlightenment. But it is dark outside, and we do not know how to proceed. Instead, we are stumbling around, bumping into one another. Suddenly, for no apparent reason, we begin dancing together. We are dancing together in a circle, where we circulate, face-to-face, around the circle in two directions. As we meet and greet one another in our dance, we are each displaying some kind of individual symbolic emblem. It is through seeing one another's signs that we recognize or realize one another. As we do this dance, a fountain of sparks erupts from the center, filling our space with light. We realize that the method of research into enlightenment that we seek is fulfilled in our dancing together.

The dream seems to be a response to the purpose of my visit, to provide consultation, as a psychology professor on the faculty at Princeton University, on creating a new program of research involving the association's membership.

In the first phase of my research with the organization, I worked with young adults attending the A.R.E. Summer Camp in the Appalachians. I attempted to see if the campers might have significant dreams if given the inspiration to seek them. I erected a special "dream tent" on the banks of White Rock Creek that ran through the camp. I invited the kids to look out for dreams that might invite them to go on a special "dream quest" in that tent. The symbolism of a womb-like tent in which a new dream might be inspired seemed to be potent medicine. A simple story combining two universal symbols out in nature—going to a sacred place and seeking spiritual inspiration—proved to have more power to evoke special dreams than any stimulation available at a typical dream laboratory.

Synchronicities were rampant. Having someone sleeping in the dream tent seemed to inspire other campers to dream about that person. We had a larger phenomenon on our hands. It was taking us from the personal to the social or cultural impact of dreams.

During this time, I had a dream. In this dream, I go to my faculty mailbox at the Princeton Psychology Department and find a letter addressed to me c/o Sundance College. In the dream I wonder, "How can a letter so mistakenly addressed find its way to me here at Princeton?" I had a vague recollection of the term *sun dance* referring to something Native American.

I was fortunate then to have the opportunity to collaborate with Dr. Robert Van de Castle, a psychiatry professor at the University of Virginia, who was consulting with the Cayce organization because of his background in the laboratory research of psychic dreams. He was an expert in Native American spirituality. He was familiar with the Native American sun dance, which the Lakota have as part of their spiritual life. In this ceremony, a circle of men dance around a central pole to which they are attached by leather tongs. They are dancing to have visions to benefit the tribe as a whole. Dancers have personal emblems or symbols on shields or shirts as part of the ceremony. The central pole becomes energized and is a source of healing. My dream of the research dance echoed this ceremony.

From these synchronicities, Robert and I created a novel experiment in group dreaming. He titled it "The Dream Helper Ceremony" as a play on the food product Hamburger Helper. It helps people get help from their dreams. It is a method, in documented fact, by which a group of people with no particular dream-work experience or knowledge can nevertheless harness their dreams reliably to achieve a practical, constructive, and creative purpose.

A group of volunteers promises to remember their dreams for the sake of a stranger in distress. The focus person's dilemma remains a secret until after the volunteers have returned with their dreams and shared them while the focus person listens. The commonalities in the dreams invariably point to the issue and demonstrate profound empathy for the stranger's distress. The dreams also mirror back light on each dreamer's own version of the human dilemma exposed, creating a healing bond for all concerned. It is certainly a research dance that sheds a lot of light.

Research into the symbolism of the Lakota sun dance revealed other cross-cultural similarities. For example, the Anglo-Saxon maypole dance is a spring celebration. Folks dance around a pole and wrap ribbons around it. A common theme here is renewal, of spring and rejuvenation. But how does dancing around a pole encourage the trees to spring forth green? It seems the symbolism springs from the same source that designed earthlings to eat the sun.

The process is via photosynthesis. Chlorophyll makes the planet green. It depends upon the carbon atom, which has twelve electrons spinning about its nucleus. In the presence of sunlight, these electrons get quite excited and jump out of orbit. It is a quantum leap that turns carbon dioxide into sugar. It is a form of sun dance that creates food out of sunlight, bringing heaven's manna to Earth. Research the symbolic theme of "twelve around one" to learn more about how heaven is mirrored on Earth.

What was it in the Mind-of-God that both engineered the photosynthesis process and prompted humans to invent the maypole dance and sun dance? Mind and matter find themselves structured by the same source. What is that source? It seems to be both within and outside, above and below.

SOME SYMBOLS TO SAMPLE

Indigenous wisdom
has inner wisdom.

A ring around a tree . . .

A dance to celebrate
the life force

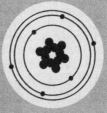

Energy from the sun
gets things moving.

SOME SYMBOLS TO SAMPLE

Dancing together has meaning.

How does a campfire draw us together?

A dream not interpreted

Clothes of our being

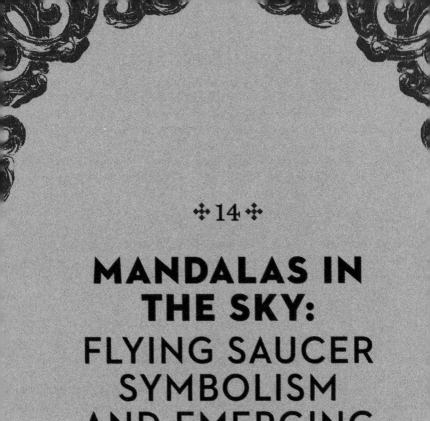

✣ 14 ✣

MANDALAS IN THE SKY:

FLYING SAUCER SYMBOLISM AND EMERGING MYTHOLOGY

THERE IS MORE TO A STORY THAN SIMPLY A CAST of characters and their personalities. There's a plot. In a story, the status quo experiences something that creates a challenge. The situation enters a state of flux, of change, of development. At some point, there is an integration of the challenge and a restoration of harmony in a new, evolved arrangement. Things are not as they were before. Soon the cycle will repeat.

The story told by humanity's symbols begins with a circle. It's an empty circle. It's a snake biting its tail. The breaking of the circle begins the cycle of creation. Duality drives the creative impulse, just as the vibration of electricity drives lightning. The story begins. The four directions create the opportunities and alternative starting points. As we travel around the circle, we accumulate experience and wisdom.

The source of this circulation of energy, originally expressed in the swastika symbol, is the Great Mystery, the Creator, or God. As creation evolves, gradually, the swastika moves from four arms to twelve and revolves around a center. The tree of life, with its many branches, expresses the completion of the lush physical creation. As life moves on, the mystery evolves. Mirror symbolism, such as the round pond into which Narcissus saw his beloved, continues the circle theme but in a new way. To say that God is within is not an unusual declaration, especially for those who've had mystical or spiritual experiences.

When we arrive at where we began, full circle, we understand the journey in a new way. Sleepwalking becomes mindful flow. Reflex becomes choice. Instinct becomes wisdom. Slaves become stewards. Creatures become cocreators. How does symbolism express this maturity of the mystery of the "I am" within?

Let's say we've "been around the block" and have visited the four corners of life, so to speak. We've integrated the medicines (lessons) from each area of life. Borrowing from the Lakota vision of the "four quarters" described in *Seven Arrows*, we will gain from the north, wisdom—what animal would represent the wisdom obtained in life? To the west is introspection—what animal might represent how introspection operates in one's life? To the south is innocence—what animal best resembles one's use of this mode of consciousness? Finally, to the east is illumination—what animal carries that medicine? Having answered these questions, imagine a circle with an image of each of those four animals, arranged with north at the top. The result would be a personal "mandala," a sacred "circle" that embraces the wholeness of the various parts.

Tibetan monks slowly create a mandala with colored sand. The mandala depicts a town with four gates. The design of the town reflects heaven, bringing heaven to Earth in a way that is complete. Opposites play with one another in this enactment. Although YouTube records it for posterity, the monks actually destroy the mandala once it's finished. The sense of permanence and perfection is then opposed by its fragile brevity as the monks sweep it away.

Today, mandala coloring books abound. The designs are pleasant to contemplate. It's peaceful to make them. For one seven-year period, I created and shared an Internet blog *The Daily Mandala*. In 2,556 different examples, it was my way of saying every morning, "The God in me waves to the God in you!"

What's going on with these mandalas?

Once again, we have to thank that most curious of persons, Carl Jung, who brought the world's attention to mandalas and made them quite popular. He would say that the mandala is the "Objective Psyche" speaking. It is saying, perhaps, something like, "Here the Infinite I *am* enjoys a mirror of momentary manifestation thanks to this specific example of being—may we continue to evolve our awareness of one another." To go from the empty circle to the mandala is a journey in consciousness.

In a very illuminating story, Dr. Jung described the evolution of the mandala imagery in the dreams of a person going through psychoanalysis with another psychiatrist. The first appearance of the mandala symbol was that the dreamer put on a *hat*. The round shape of the hat and its relationship to a crown gave the hat its mandala quality. Other round things observed in later dreams were a coin and a ball. The mandala has a center, a focus, and radiates from there, such as in the person's dream of a flower, a fountain, and a shooting star. There is often the suggestion of rotation, or going around a circle, as in the patient's dream of a clock and of a circle dance. Finally, mandala imagery has reference to four or square, as in a dream of a tree in the center of a square garden, and of four people sitting at a round table.

The mandala is a symbol of getting it all together through the integration of the opposites. It is a soul print upon the human mind of the universal source of our design, uniquely expressed in an individual life. The ancient mystery of "squaring the circle" pertains to the task of bringing the boundless Heaven to Earth in its bounded four quarters. How might one create, with the sacred geometer's compass and ruler, a square that matches a circle's exact area? The impossibility of this task mirrored to Pythagoreans a spiritual truth: It is not possible to manifest in the four quarters of a lifetime the full scope of the immortal soul.

Today's fascination with mandalas is some proof of the symbol's continuing vitality. Dr. Jung saw yet another dimension to the mandala, based upon the public's fascination with flying saucers. When flying saucers came to wide public attention during the 1950s, Dr.

Jung noted that whether or not physical evidence confirmed their existence, it was clear that *folks wanted to believe* in flying saucers. To him, this psychological reality had spiritual implications of an emerging new mythology.

The exciting, stimulating, inspiring fantasy that one day flying saucers might land and introduce us to a new super being may be a thin disguise for an emerging new religion. The evolving myth has God transforming from an Old Man in the Sky to something alive within our hearts and minds. The intelligence that created the universe has also designed the mind that can perceive the creation and, ultimately, the Creator. Consciousness is fulfilling its role by evolving to recognize its ultimate Source. The mandala sighs, "Ah, so!"

SOME SYMBOLS TO SAMPLE

It's a whole wide world.

An expression of presence

God's autograph in nature

Everything is in order.

SOME SYMBOLS TO SAMPLE

A higher intelligence
reveals itself.

A spiritual view of all
that is

Finding our way to the center

A mirror of the
creative forces

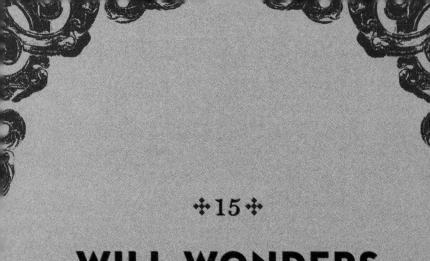

✦ 15 ✦

WILL WONDERS NEVER CEASE? DREAMS AND THE SYMBOLIC LIFE

A SPIRITUAL FRAMEWORK FOR CONTEMPLATING life provides a very helpful context for engaging dream work and exploring symbolism. Perhaps the most general trend today in that regard would be that of integral philosophy. It has many contributors: the Indian philosopher Sri Aurobindo, the psychiatrist Carl Jung, the mystic-psychic Edgar Cayce, and the contemporary scholar Ken Wilber are perhaps the four most influential of many who have helped shape this movement in thought. In this view, consciousness is the driver of evolution, which occurs through the integration of new awareness into current consciousness. Creation seems to intend to become conscious of itself. This dynamic shows up in later-stage human development as the drive to expand awareness to include a feeling of intimate oneness with all that is.

The dynamic duality of spirit living in physicality, of godlike beings having to exist and get along with mortal humans, creates a typical path of developmental challenges. A child's spirit gets shut down in order to produce a socialized adult. In later life, adversities force suppressed qualities out of hiding and thereby evolve consciousness. Dreaming is a state of consciousness not limited by the dualistic focus of physical, sensory consciousness. Dreaming is a resource that serves the goal of evolution of consciousness in the context of the physical/social constraints humans confront.

In dreams we view our daytime experience from the vantage point of Mind-of-God. This vantage point provides correction, either encouragement or admonishment, in the form of compensatory experiences that help to bring us back closer to the mark. The purpose of the dreams is to help us empathize with that Mind-of-God perspective, so we can use it to help us in our daily lives. Empathizing with the symbols in the dream is quite consistent with the purpose of dreaming.

We can always look up the "meaning" of a dream symbol by doing a quick Internet search or looking in our favorite symbol dictionary. There we'll find words that will attach to the symbol and further spark our imagination. The best use of such research tools is to treat their ideas as suggestions to the imagination. Don't let the magic spell of words create the illusion of a symbol's fixed meaning. Use definitions as arrows pointing out directions to explore in the quest for an empathic relationship with the symbol.

There is a way to create a personal dream symbol dictionary. First, collect a couple dozen symbols to explore. Find or create a picture of each one and seal it in an opaque envelope. Once a week, pick an envelope at random, not knowing the symbol inside. Make an intuitive heart connection with the unseen symbol inside the envelope, and then imagine the symbol stimulating soul memories. Relax into the breathing, and pray that the next breath will bring a memory that will provide a personal perspective on something the symbol is trying to express. Record the memory, and do some journaling about the "lesson" the memory contains for you. Then open the envelope, discover the symbol, and meditate on what the memory has to teach about that symbol. For the next couple of days, watch for synchronicities to direct attention to further insights. Invite the symbol to lunch! Let the inner child use the imagination to play with the symbol. Using improvisational writing as a medium of exploration, one might have a dialogue with a symbol. Ask the symbol, "What would you like from me? How can I help you become my friend? How would you handle this situation?"

It is safe to assume that a symbol in a dream has something to do with the dreamer. Suppose a person dreamed, "I discover a snake under my bed."

In dream interpretation, we generally start with the assumption that all components of a dream mirror parts of the dreamer. I have found it helpful, therefore, to rewrite the dream in a special way: "I have myself discovered a snake *part of myself* under the bed *part of myself*." This rewriting of the dream makes it easier to meditate on the symbols' suggestive qualities within myself. The rewritten dream text is now in a language that mirrors how dream symbols come from within.

It is important to be sincere and invested in the investigation of a symbol, as the teacher appears only when the student is ready. The study of symbolism, if it is to be personally meaningful and constructive, is truly an adventure in growth and discovery, just like a flower blossoming. It's hard to understand the river's wisdom from the shore; better to step into the flow. Make an offering to the spirit of the symbol, for example, as an expression of good faith that the wisdom gained will be applied. Symbolism is not a spectator sport. Taking proactive steps to court the favor of the symbol creates an appropriate atmosphere of adventure.

I'll share a final personal story that perhaps will answer the question, "How do I know I'm not just making all this stuff up?"

When I began my research with the dream tent at the A.R.E. Summer Camp, I did not know how to proceed in a sacred manner so that the spirit would be alive. I decided to meditate and to do so with the assumption that I know what I'm doing. After the meditation, I walked down to the creek and began an improvised ritual of finding the sacred *center*, circumscribing the *protective circle* around it, and establishing the *four corners*. I painted a picture of the thusly sanctified ground. Then I took a nap. I awoke with an image of a beetle in the middle of a circle. I then noticed that in my painting, where I had drawn a circle for the tambourine I had used in my ritual, there now sat a colorful Japanese beetle! After I erected the tent, I went for a walk, only to stumble down, face-first, into a bush full of Japanese beetles! It was uncanny. The immensity of this encounter shocked me.

The iridescent, golden green scarabs shouted in unison that my efforts with the dream tent would have lasting, transformative value. It proved true, both for me personally and the future of dream research.

Such synchronicities create the magic by which symbols come alive and ring true. A new feeling of connection with the universe arises, within and around. The boundary between psyche and soma begins to dissolve. Opposites attract to integrate and create anew. Bare feet sprout natural shoes to caress the ground with a confident embrace. Wisdom and innocence coexist, and life overflows with wonder—from just a little symbolism.

SOME SYMBOLS TO SAMPLE

To sleep, perchance
to dream

Is it poisonous or not?

Don't let it bug you!

A collage of the
author's symbols

SOME SYMBOLS TO SAMPLE

There's a rhythm to everything.

A journey is a story unfolding.

Following the evidence

A collage of the author's animals

INDEX

A

Adventure, nature and, 49–50
Animal symbolism, 54–61
  bears, 57–58
  exploring, 58–59
  Native American teachings, 57
  recognizable symbols, 60–61
  "symbol-on-the-brain" process, 55
  turtles, 56
Archetypes, 21
Asclepius, miracles of, 40–41
Association for Research and
  Enlightenment, 9, 95–96
Aurobindo, Sri, 111

B

Bears, symbolism of, 57–58
Body
  dreams forewarning disease, 41–42
  eye symbolism, 74, 77
  hand symbolism, 73–74, 77
  head/face symbolism, 74–75, 76
  heart symbolism, 72–73, 76, 77
  house symbolizing, 42–43
  made in image of God, 71
  miracles of Asclepius and, 40–41
  as mirror of creation, 71–75
  recognizable symbols, 44–45, 76–77
  as temple, 38–45
Breathing, 24, 26–27, 72, 113

C

Campbell, Joseph, 21
Cayce, Charles Thomas, 95
Cayce, Edgar, 20, 95, 111
Circle(s)
  archetype of, 21
  creation mystery and, 17–21, 24, 25–27,
    103–104
  divinely suggestive aspects, 20–21
  four directions on earth and, 32–35
  mandalas and, 103–107

protective, 114
  snake biting tail to form, 19–20, 21, 103
Compass directions, 32–33, 36, 64
Consciousness
  birth of, 27
  creation and, 18, 31
  intuitive methods of expanding, 9
  meditation and, 24–25, 26, 42
  separation and, 25–26
  symbolism expanding, 10–11, 13–14, 42,
    49–51
  symbols of inner nature and, 46–53
Creation, 103–104
  Adam, Eve and biting into apple, 25–26,
    27, 74
  body as mirror of, 71–75
  circle symbolism and, 17–21, 24
  four directions on earth and, 32–34, 35
  mirroring the Creator, 71
  ouroboros symbol and, 19–20
  of self-awareness, 25–27
  separation and, 25–26
  symbolism of myths, 17–21
  unity of, 13, 81–83

D

Dance of evaporating raindrops, 34–35,
  47–48
Directions on earth, 30–35
Dreams
  about shoes, 1–3, 4, 10, 12–13
  about smoking in church, 39–40
  animal symbolism and, 57–59
  body as temple, body symbols and, 39–43
  Cayce location experiments, 95–98
  daydreams, 51, 55
  dictionary of symbols, 112–113
  dream tent experiment, 96–97, 114–115
  empathy in, 10, 98, 112
  inspiring empathy for unconscious mind, 10
  integral philosophy and, 111
  interpreting/investigating, 111–115
  Jung on, 87–88
  mandala imagery in, 106
  Mind-of-God perspective, 10, 112

ABOUT THE AUTHOR

HENRY REED, PhD, is a visionary psychologist, an "academic shaman," an artist of dreams and dreamwork, and an innovator of intuitive methodologies of creativity. His published books include *Awakening Your Psychic Powers*, *The Intuitive Heart*, and *Edgar Cayce on Channeling Your Higher Self*. Henry was an assistant professor of psychology at Princeton University and served as a research consultant to the C.G. Jung Dream Laboratory in Zürich, Switzerland. He currently serves as director of the Edgar Cayce Institute for Intuitive Studies. His blogs include dailymandala.blogspot.com and 1REED. He lives in the mountains of Mouth of Wilson, VA.

IMAGE CREDITS

ALAMY © Pictorial Press Ltd: 100 bottom left & top right

COURTESY THE AUTHOR 108 top right, 116 bottom right, 117 bottom right

DEPOSITPHOTOS © alvaroc: 29 top left; © artistique: 69 top left, 84 top left; © baavli: 77 bottom left; © Chantall: 116 bottom left; © glossygirl: 28 bottom left; © chekat: 5 top left; © i_panki: 077 top right; © I.Petrovic: 60 bottom right; © Inna_af: 77 top left; © JRMurray76: 93 top left; © Kilroy: 69 top right; © koya979: 92 top left; © Krisdog: 28 top right; © kvasay: 61 top left; © kytalpa: 51 bottom left; © lavalova: 15 top right; © lefpap: 44 bottom left; © leremy: 85 top left; © levente: 61 bottom right; © Mariannette: 61 top right; © MSSA: 21; © OlhaM: 61 bottom right; © PiXXart: 28 top left; © Ravennk: 36 top right; © RedKoala: 29 bottom left, 52 top left, bottom left & right, 76 top left; © Seamartini: 36 top left; © skarin1: 116 top left; © spiral_media: 69 bottom right; © tuulijumala: 29 top right; © xochicalco: 76 bottom left

DREAMSTIME © Barbulat: 68 top right; © Faitotoro: 5 bottom left, 52 top right, 101 bottom right; © Nipponsan: 15 bottom right, 68 bottom right

ISTOCKPHOTO © amtitus: 37; © appleuzr: 53 bottom left & top right; © azureforest: 108 bottom left; © Bakai: 53 top left; © Barbulat: 28 bottom right, 68 top left; © Alex Belomlinsky: 44 top right, 60 bottom left, 76 bottom right, 117 top left; © Keith Bishop: 85 top right; © chuvipro: 109 top right; © Grant Cottrell: 60 top right; © duncan1890: 85 bottom left; © epic11: 84 bottom left; © Suat Gürsözlü: 77 bottom right; © Kathy Konkle: 92 top left; © kumdinpitak: 117 top right; © martin951: 93 bottom left; © Craig McCausland: 45 top right; © mokhtari: 46 bottom left; © nadyaillyustrator: 60 top left; © Konstantin Nikiteev: 117 bottom left; © Panptys: 109 top left; © Rakdee: 29 bottom right, 53 bottom right; © Larry Rains: 44 bottom right; © Frank Ramspott: 101 top right; © Anna Rassadnikova: 44 top left; © rhoon: 109 bottom right; © ruthyoel: 93 top right; © TheModernCanvas: 46 bottom right; © Adan Thoth: 109 bottom left; © ty4ina: 5 bottom right; © Virtaa: 101 bottom left; © xochicalco: 45 top left

SHUTTERSTOCK © Everett Historical: 100 top left; © Mary Frost: 15 top left; © general-fmv: 100 bottom right; © LWY Partnership: 5 top right; © Tim the Finn: 92 bottom left; © Utro_na_more: cover & throughout

COURTESY WIKIMEDIA FOUNDATION: 84 top, 93 bottom; Daderot: 85 bottom right; Freer Gallery of Art: 108 top right; Alejandro Linares Garcia: 76 top right; Wellcome Library, London: 101 top left